POC
MAN

Haynes

Pollok Library
Pollok Civic Realm
27 Cowglen Road
Glasgow G53 2EN

BREATHE DEEPLY

*When feeling pressured, breathe
in slowly through the nose
and out through the mouth.
You will soon begin to feel relaxed*

Published in August 2011

British Library Cataloguing-in-Publication Data:
A catalogue record for this book is available from
the British Library

ISBN 978 0 85733 044 4

Published by Haynes Publishing,
Sparkford, Yeovil, Somerset BA22 7JJ, UK
Tel: 01963 442030 Fax: 01963 440001
Int. tel: +44 1963 442030 Int. fax: +44 1963 440001
Email: sales@haynes.co.uk
Website: www.haynes.co.uk

Haynes North America, Inc.,
861 Lawrence Drive, Newbury Park
California 91320, USA

Design and layout by Richard Parsons

All photographs courtesy of Getty Images

All statistics and dates correct as of June 2011

Printed in the USA

The Author

This is the fourth book Nick Judd ... have produced together.
Tim is delighted to see a Southampton player finally mentioned. Nick's
beloved Swindon Town are still awaiting their first representative.

WORLD FOOTBALL STARS
CONTENTS

TOP 50   6

From exciting tricksters
to reliable stoppers and
everything in between,
we've assembled the
world's greatest footballers

XABI ALONSO 8

NICOLAS ANELKA 10

KARIM BENZEMA 11

DIMITAR BERBATOV 12

IKER CASILLAS 13

MAROUANE CHAMAKH 14

GIORGIO CHIELLINI 15

ASHLEY COLE 16

DANIELE DE ROSSI 18

DIEGO 19

LANDON DONOVAN 20

DIDIER DROGBA 21

EDIN DZEKO 22

MICHAEL ESSIEN 23

SAMUEL ETO'O 24

LUIS FABIANO 26

CESC FABREGAS 27

RIO FERDINAND 28

DIEGO FORLAN 30

STEVEN GERRARD 32

ALBERTO GILARDINO 33

MAREK HAMSIK 34

KLASS-JAN HUNTELAAR 35

ZLATAN IBRAHIMOVIC 36

ANDRES INIESTA 37

KAKA 38

PHILIPP LAHM 39

POCKET
MANUAL

Teams and players, facts and figures

WORLD FOOTBALL STARS

FRANK LAMPARD	40
DIEGO LUGANO	42
MAICON	43
JAVIER MASCHERANO	44
FLORENT MALOUDA	45
LIONEL MESSI	46
DIEGO MILITO	48
NANI	50
GERARD PIQUE	52
FRANCK RIBERY	54
ARJEN ROBBEN	55
CRISTIANO RONALDO	56
WAYNE ROONEY	58
BASTIAN SCHWEINSTEIGER	60
WESLEY SNEIJDER	61
JOHN TERRY	62
CARLOS TEVEZ	64
FERNANDO TORRES	65
YAYA TOURE	66
ROBIN VAN PERSIE	67
NEMANJA VIDIC	68
DAVID VILLA	69
XAVI	70

NEW TO YOU 72

Keep your eyes on
these international
bright young things
in 2011 and beyond

LEGENDS 106

Proving age is no
barrier, here's a handful
of household names
still going strong

GLOBAL GATHERING

Europe and South America are famous for producing the best footballers in the game, but football is far reaching. More and more stars are emerging from all four corners of the world...

① USA

Morocco ①

Ivory Coast ②①

Ghana

① Cameroon

④ Brazil

② Uruguay

④ Argentina

TOP 50

Map labels:
- ① Sweden
- ④ Holland
- ⑥ England
- ② Germany
- ① Slovakia
- ④ France
- ① Serbia
- ① Bosnia
- ① Bulgaria
- ② Portugal
- ③ Italy
- ⑧ Spain

Spain	⑧	Uruguay	②
England	⑥	Bosnia	①
Argentina	④	Bulgaria	①
Brazil	④	Cameroon	①
France	④	Ghana	①
Holland	④	Morocco	①
Italy	③	Serbia	①
Germany	②	Slovakia	①
Ivory Coast	②	Sweden	①
Portugal	②	USA	①

XABI ALONSO

DOB:	**25.11.1981**
NATIONALITY:	**Spain**
POSITION:	**Midfield**
HEIGHT:	**183cm**

CURRENT CLUB:
Real Madrid

PREVIOUS CLUBS:
**Liverpool, Elbar (loan),
Real Sociedad**

When the defensive midfielder joined Liverpool from Real Sociedad in 2004, few in the UK had heard of the Spaniard. However, his ability to open up the opposition with his vision and range of passing, as well as his spectacular goals (see right) made him an Anfield favourite and prompted Real Madrid to sign him for £30million in 2009. He left England after winning the Champions League in 2005, the European Super Cup the same year and the FA Cup and Community Shield in 2006. The Spanish international was also part of the *Furia Roja* squad that won Euro 2008 and the 2010 World Cup.

TOP
50

DID YOU KNOW?

Alonso, whose dad won the Spanish League twice in successive seasons with Real Sociedad in the early 1980s, scored from 67 yards in 2005/06 during an FA Cup third-round tie against Luton Town at Kenilworth Road. He proved it was no fluke when, a year later, he scored from 61 yards in a game against Newcastle United, which is still the longest strike in Premier League history.

NICOLAS
ANELKA

DOB:	14.03.1979
CLUB:	Chelsea
NATIONALITY:	France
POSITION:	Forward
HEIGHT:	185cm

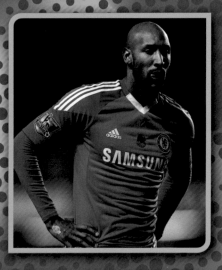

In 1997, Anelka first left Paris St Germain with "great potential", according to his coach. Little did Anelka's coach know how successful the striker would be at so many different clubs. He joined Arsenal aged 17, won a league and cup double and scored 28 goals in 90 appearances. He was Real Madrid's record signing in 1999 at £22.3million. He returned to Paris, from where he joined Liverpool on loan before Kevin Keegan made him Manchester City's record buy at £13million. In 2006, after a spell at Turkish club Fenerbahce, Bolton also smashed their transfer high. He left to join Chelsea, his eighth club, in 2008, where he has won a league title and two FA Cups.

KARIM
BENZEMA

DOB: 19.12.1987

CLUB: Real Madrid

NATIONALITY: France

POSITION: Forward

HEIGHT: 183cm

It is no coincidence that when Olympique Lyonnais won seven consecutive Ligue 1 titles between 2002 and 2008, striker Benzema was involved in more than half of them. The French international stepped up from the club's academy in January 2005 and made the world sit up and take notice in 2007/08, scoring 32 goals in 52 games in all competitions. He finished the campaign as Ligue 1's top scorer and player of the year, then underlined his talent by scoring 23 goals in 48 games the following season. A French international, Benzema signed a six-year deal at Real Madrid in 2009.

DIMITAR BERBATOV

DOB:	**30.01.1981**
CLUB:	**Manchester United**
NATIONALITY:	**Bulgaria**
POSITION:	**Forward**
HEIGHT:	**188cm**

Often criticised as a result of his languid style, Berbatov has been finding the form for Manchester United that made him so prolific at Tottenham Hotspur and Bayer Leverkusen. An expert finisher with the ability to play with his back to goal and bring others into the game, the six-times winner of the Bulgarian Player of the Year Award at first failed to find the net on a regular basis following his £30million move to United in September 2008. Yet he began the 2010/11 season by scoring seven goals in seven starts and ended the season joint top goalscorer in the Premier League with 21. He scored 69 goals in 154 games in Germany and added 27 in two years at Spurs.

IKER
CASILLAS

DOB:	**20.05.1981**
CLUB:	**Real Madrid**
NATIONALITY:	**Spain**
POSITION:	**Goalkeeper**
HEIGHT:	**184cm**

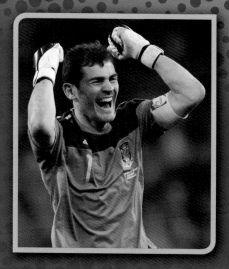

Captain of the Spanish national team, for whom he has more than 110 caps, Casillas led the *Furia Roja* to their first European Championship triumph in 44 years, in 2008. Two years later, the skipper lifted Spain's first-ever World Cup. He boasts tremendous speed, agility and quick reflexes and in February 2009 he passed Paco Buyo's club record of 454 appearances in goal for Real Madrid. The goalkeeper was handed his first start in 1998/99 and made the no.1 jersey his own within a year. Days after his 19th birthday he became the youngest goalkeeper to play in and win a Champions League final.

MAROUANE CHAMAKH

DOB:	10.01.1984
CLUB:	Arsenal
NATIONALITY:	Morocco
POSITION:	Forward
HEIGHT:	188cm

Arsenal manager Arsene Wenger courted striker Chamakh for 12 months before finally landing the Moroccan's services in May 2010. It was worth the wait. Although he ended the season in and out of the Gunners' side, in 2010 Chamakh became the first player across Europe to find the net in six consecutive Champions League matches. He joined Arsenal from Bordeaux, for whom he made his debut and helped win a league and cup double in 2008/09. In his last season, 2009/10, he didn't miss a league match. He is a strong runner and his work ethic makes him popular with the fans.

GIORGIO
CHIELLINI

DOB:	14.08.1984
CLUB:	Juventus
NATIONALITY:	Italy
POSITION:	Defence
HEIGHT:	192cm

A dominant aerial presence and an impressive man-marker, Juventus centre-back Giorgio Chiellini was once described by former AC Milan boss Carlo Ancelotti as "the best defender in Italy" and he has been voted Serie A's finest in 2008/09 and 2009/10. He started his career as a left-back at Livorno, then Fiorentina. He joined Juventus in 2005 and in 2006/07 Chiellini was moved into the centre by then coach Didier Deschamps. Chiellini and his defensive unit conceded just 30 goals in Serie B and he made the position his own, his strength and leadership skills making him a formidable player.

ASHLEY COLE

DOB: 20.12.1980

NATIONALITY: England

POSITION: Defence

HEIGHT: 172cm

CURRENT CLUB:
Chelsea

PREVIOUS CLUBS:
Crystal Palace (loan),
Arsenal

ENGLAND

One of the best left-backs in the world and England's most-capped black player, Cole is just 5ft 8in, but his pace, fearless attitude and toughness in the tackle more than make up for it. He doesn't think twice about throwing himself into 50/50 challenges while he can frustrate opponents with his persistence and guile. He's dangerous going forward, too. He started his career as a striker in Arsenal's youth academy and still loves rampaging down the left touchline. At Arsenal he won two league titles and added a third following his move to Chelsea in 2006.

DID YOU KNOW?

When Chelsea lifted the FA Cup in 2010 following a 1-0 win against Portsmouth, Cole became the first footballer to win six FA Cup winners' medals. His first came in 2002 with Arsenal. He won it again a year later before scoring in the penalty shoot-out that secured victory in 2005. He won the trophy in his first season at Chelsea, in 2007 and added consecutive medals to his collection with wins in 2009 and 2010.

DANIELE
DE ROSSI

DOB:	**24.07.1983**
CLUB:	**AS Roma**
NATIONALITY:	**Italy**
POSITION:	**Midfield**
HEIGHT:	**182cm**

De Rossi is a deep-lying midfielder who can break up attacks and get forward with pace and shoot from distance, which with his commitment and will to win makes the Italian a formidable opponent. Born and bred in Rome, De Rossi has enjoyed a successful route to the top. He was a European Champion with Italy's U21s in 2004 and a bronze-medal winner at the Olympics in Athens the same summer. A few weeks later he scored on his full international debut in a 2-1 win against Norway. A Serie A runner-up five times, De Rossi is yet to win Italy's top prize.

DIEGO

DOB:	28.02.1985
CLUB:	VfL Wolfsburg
NATIONALITY:	Brazil
POSITION:	Midfield
HEIGHT:	175cm

With nine seasons under his belt already it's hard to believe Brazilian playmaker Diego – who joined Wolfsburg in 2010 – is only 26. He played in the Copa Libertadores final, Brazil's showpiece knockout tournament, aged 17, and made his international debut, for Brazil, in 2003. A move to FC Porto followed in 2004 before he joined German giants Werder Bremen two years later. There, he successfully linked midfield and attack and his creativity saw him become hot property. He helped the *Green-Whites* lift the German Cup before joining Italian giants Juventus in 2009.

LANDON DONOVAN

DOB:	04.03.1982
CLUB:	LA Galaxy
NATIONALITY:	USA
POSITION:	Midfield/Forward
HEIGHT:	173cm

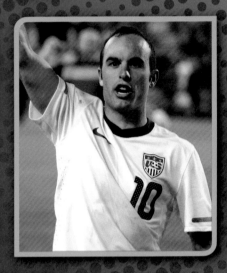

Donovan is America's all-time top scorer, with 45 goals. The Californian has also smashed the 100-cap barrier for his country (128 and still counting) and has proved himself outside of the USA's Major League Soccer, for whom he plays for LA Galaxy. He enjoyed a successful loan move to Bayern Munich in 2009 before a stint at Everton, where he scored twice in 13 appearances and won the club's Player of the Month award in January 2010. That summer, at the World Cup, he scored twice as the USA topped their group for the first time since 1930 before going out in the last 16.

DIDIER DROGBA

DOB:	11.03.1978
CLUB:	Chelsea
NATIONALITY:	Ivory Coast
POSITION:	Forward
HEIGHT:	180cm

When Didier Drogba ended his first season with French side Guincamp with three goals in 11 games, few would have predicted his meteoric rise. However, the following year he scored 17 in 34 and moved to Marseille, for whom he scored 18 in 35 appearances in 2003/04. His powerful style and eye for goal saw him move to Chelsea for £24million in 2004, where he has won three league titles, three FA Cups and two League Cups and has scored almost 100 goals – more than any other foreign Chelsea player. He is current captain and all-time highest scorer for the Ivory Coast.

EDIN DZEKO

DOB: 17.03.1986

CLUB: Manchester City

NATIONALITY: Bosnia-Herzegovina

POSITION: Forward

HEIGHT: 193cm

In June 2007 striker Dzeko played for his country against Malta in a match that would transform his career. He was watched by a Wolfsburg scout who had been alerted by the striker's 13 goals in 30 games at Czech side FK Teplice. The Germans were impressed. By the end of 2008/09 he'd won the German title, formed the best striker partnership in Bundesliga history with team-mate Grafite and scored 35 goals in 65 appearances. Dzeko hit 61 goals in his first 100 Bundesliga games to overtake Wolfsburg's record scorer, Diego Klimowicz (57). He moved to Manchester City in January 2011.

MICHAEL
ESSIEN

DOB:	03.12.1982
CLUB:	Chelsea
NATIONALITY:	Ghana
POSITION:	Midfield
HEIGHT:	177cm

Essien returned to action during the 2010/11 season after missing most of the previous campaign – and the 2010 World Cup in South Africa – with injury. Both Chelsea and Ghana missed his energy, his acute passing and surges into the opposition area. The Ghanaian won consecutive league titles with Olympique Lyonnais in France in 2004 and 2005 and was voted French Player of the Year before moving to Chelsea in 2005. He has won two league titles, two FA Cups and a League Cup winners' medal in London. Not bad for a player rejected by Manchester United as a youngster...

SAMUEL ETO'O

DOB: 10.03.1981

NATIONALITY: Cameroon

POSITION: Forward

HEIGHT: 178cm

CURRENT CLUB:
Inter Milan

PREVIOUS CLUBS:
Barcelona, Mallorca, Mallorca
(loan), Espanyol (loan),
Leganes (loan), Real Madrid

The winner of more honours than any other African footballer, the Cameroon legend admits he watches all kinds of football on television to help him identify new tactics. It works. He bagged a league, cup and European Cup treble with Barcelona in 2008/09 before moving to Inter Milan that summer, where he won the treble in his first season. Eto'o scored 54 goals in 133 appearances after joining Mallorca in 2000 – making him the club's record scorer. At Barca's Nou Camp, he won two Champions League titles, three league winners' medals and scored 108 goals in 145 matches.

TOP 50

DID YOU KNOW?

Samuel Eto'o loves breaking records. In 2010, he became the first player to win two European Continental Trebles following his consecutive achievements with Barcelona and Inter Milan. Along with Dutchman Clarence Seedorf he's one of two players to win the Champions League with three separate teams, although he was on loan at Mallorca from parent club Real Madrid when he picked up his first winners' medal in 2002. He's also the all-time leading scorer in the Africa Cup of Nations, with 18 goals.

LUIS
FABIANO

TOP 50

DOB:	08.11.1980
CLUB:	Sevilla
NATIONALITY:	Brazil
POSITION:	Forward
HEIGHT:	186cm

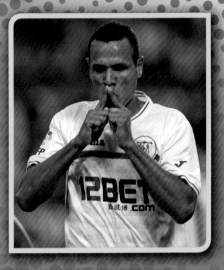

Before joining current employers Sevilla, 'O Fabuloso' notched 61 goals in 85 games for São Paulo in Brazil thanks to his strength, speed and shooting accuracy. He couldn't find the same consistency during a year-long spell at FC Porto, but Fabiano regained his scoring touch in Spain. He averages a goal every other game and in his five-year stay he's won two UEFA Cups, the UEFA Super Cup and two Copa Del Reys. He made his international debut for Brazil in 2003. He top scored in the 2009 Confederations Cup with five and bagged another nine in 2010 World Cup qualifying matches.

CESC FABREGAS

DOB:	04.05.1987
CLUB:	Arsenal
NATIONALITY:	Spain
POSITION:	Midfield
HEIGHT:	175cm

A product of the *Can Barca* academy that produced fellow Spanish stars Xavi and Andres Iniesta, Fabregas boasts similar technique, vision, the ability to unlock defences and an eye for goal. The youngest player to represent Arsenal, aged 16 years and 177 days, and their youngest-ever goalscorer, he's now in his seventh season and leads the team with distinction, although he continues to be linked with a move back to Barcelona. A Spanish international, he scored twice and made three assists in Euro 2008 and set up the extra-time winner for Iniesta in the 2010 World Cup final against Holland.

RIO
FERDINAND

DOB: 07.11.1978

NATIONALITY: England

POSITION: Defence

HEIGHT: 195cm

CURRENT CLUB:
Manchester United

PREVIOUS CLUBS:
Leeds United, Bournemouth
(loan), West Ham United

ENGLAND

The former England captain has been back to his imperial best
in 2011. After missing large chunks of the 2009/10 season – as
well as the World Cup in South Africa – through injury, Ferdinand
has returned to form for club and country. Solid at the back as
England raced to the top of their Euro 2011 qualifying group, he
also kept four clean sheets upon his league return in 2010/11
and impressed as United collected a record 19th league title
and reached the final of the Champions League. Ferdinand's
finest year to date came in 2008 when he captained United
to a League and European double.

TOP
50

DID YOU KNOW?

When Ferdinand was made England skipper in February 2010 he became the 107th player in Three Lions' history to lead his country. In total, Ferdinand captained England on seven occasions. Billy Wright and Bobby Moore both captained England on 90 occasions, more than any other England skippers.

DIEGO
FORLAN

DOB:	19.05.1979
NATIONALITY:	Uruguay
POSITION:	Forward
HEIGHT:	181cm

CURRENT CLUB:
Atletico Madrid

PREVIOUS CLUBS:
Villarreal, Manchester
United, Independiente

The player voted star of the 2010 World Cup (see right)
scored 69 goals in his first 106 games for Atletico Madrid,
beating the 54 he scored in the same number of games for
previous club Villarreal. Not surprisingly, he has twice won
the European Golden Boot (for most goals in a season),
one of eight players to do so. Hailing from a footballing
family – his father, grandfather and brother all played at
various levels – Forlan started his career at Independiente
before joining Manchester United, where he scored 17
goals and became a fan favourite.

DID YOU KNOW?

Forlan junior once admitted his father loved to brag about having played in two World Cups compared to his one, but that all changed in South Africa in 2010. Forlan not only competed in the tournament for the second time, he scored five goals, helped Uruguay to the semi-finals for the first time in 40 years and was awarded the Golden Ball as the tournament's best player – the fourth South American to receive the award.

STEVEN GERRARD

DOB:	**30.05.1980**
CLUB:	**Liverpool**
NATIONALITY:	**England**
POSITION:	**Midfield**
HEIGHT:	**185cm**

ENGLAND

The dynamic England midfielder has been one of the *Three Lions'* most consistent performers since the World Cup in South Africa. He scored twice in a friendly against Hungary and impressed as the *Three Lions* got their Euro 2012 qualifying campaign off to a winning start, with victories against Bulgaria and Switzerland. A one-club man, Gerrard, now club captain and about to enter his 14th season, has won nine trophies with Liverpool. His main attribute is the ability to turn matches with crucial goals, like his winner in the Champions League against Olympiakos in September 2004, and again in the FA Cup final against West Ham United in 2006.

ALBERTO GILARDINO

DOB:	05.07.1982
CLUB:	Fiorentina
NATIONALITY:	Italy
POSITION:	Forward
HEIGHT:	184cm

ITALIA

FIGC

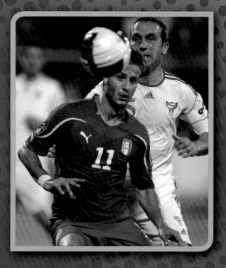

Italian striker Gilardino enjoyed his best year in international colours in 2009, scoring six goals in nine games. His club record hasn't been bad either. His pace, heading and ability to use both feet has seen him fire more than 45 goals in the last two seasons for Fiorentina, where he has struck up a good partnership with Romanian forward Adrian Mutu. It looks as though current Italy boss Cesare Prandelli gets the best out of Gilardino. He was the striker's boss at Fiorentina and Parma, where he scored 55 goals in three seasons and was voted Italian and Serie A Football of the Year before joining AC Milan in 2005, with whom he won the Champions League in 2007.

MAREK HAMSIK

DOB:	**27.07.1987**
CLUB:	**Napoli**
NATIONALITY:	**Slovakia**
POSITION:	**Midfield**
HEIGHT:	**184cm**

Slovakia coach Vladimir Weiss describes the talented Hamsik as "a gifted, world-class player". Weiss gave him the captain's arm band in October 2009 and the youngster has led by example, helping the nation qualify for their first World Cup in history, in 2010. Hamsik joined Serie A club Napoli in 2007 and has become a key player in the centre of midfield. He boasts the ability to score from range and create opportunities for others, while his work ethic and willingness to track back and protect his defence have made him a hit with the fans.

KLASS-JAN HUNTELAAR

DOB:	12.08.1983
CLUB:	Schalke
NATIONALITY:	Holland
POSITION:	Forward
HEIGHT:	185cm

KNVB

'The Hunter' joined Real Madrid in 2009 and scored eight goals in 20 games, but he failed to settle in Spain. Seven goals in 25 matches followed at AC Milan and Huntelaar boasted a similar record following his move to Schalke, for whom he scored six times in his first seven games. He found the net twice on his international debut in 2006 and at the time of writing, he was joint-leading goalscorer in Euro 2012 qualifying. He netted 76 goals in 92 league matches for Ajax between 2005 and 2009, making him the most consistent Dutch striker in recent history.

ZLATAN
IBRAHIMOVIC

DOB:	03.10.1981
CLUB:	AC Milan (loan)
NATIONALITY:	Sweden
POSITION:	Forward
HEIGHT:	194cm

Swedish striker Ibrahimovic divides opinion. Some say his swagger, impressive control and finishing make him one of the world's best. To others he's inconsistent and yet to prove his talent on the biggest stage. Either way, he boasts an incredible goal record and in 2009 he commanded the second-highest transfer fee in history – £56.5million – when he moved from Inter Milan to Barcelona. At Inter, he scored 57 goals in 88 league appearances including 25 in 2008/09, making him Serie A's top scorer. He spent 2010/11 on loan at AC Milan, where he won the Serie A league title and averaged a goal every other game.

ANDRES INIESTA

DOB:	11.05.1984
CLUB:	Barcelona
NATIONALITY:	Spain
POSITION:	Midfield
HEIGHT:	170cm

Andres Iniesta and Xavi make up one of the most gifted and thrilling midfield duos in world football. Both can find spaces and gaps others can't. Iniesta's best moment in club colours came in 2008 when, with Barcelona, he not only won an unprecedented treble, he did it in style. After the Champions League final, defeated Manchester United striker Wayne Rooney declared Iniesta "the best player in the world". That summer, the Spaniard helped his country win Euro 2008. In 2009 he set up 59 goals at Barca. In 2010 Iniesta scored the decisive goal to win the World Cup. A year later he won a unique treble of winners' medals including the league, the Spanish Super Cup and Champions League.

KAKA

DOB:	**22.04.1982**
CLUB:	**Real Madrid**
NATIONALITY:	**Brazil**
POSITION:	**Midfield**
HEIGHT:	**186cm**

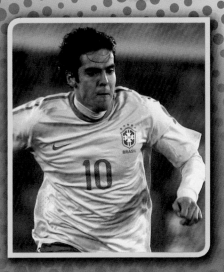

Graceful, intelligent and boasting great technique, Kaka has the ability to split a defence with a pass or score from range. These qualities saw him briefly become the world's most expensive player when he moved from AC Milan to Real Madrid, only for his fee of £56million to be topped by Cristiano Ronaldo days later. The Brazilian international is looking to repeat his Milan achievements at the Bernabeu. He won Serie A, Champions League and World Club Cup winners' medals and hit a career-best of 16 goals in 2008/09. The former Ballon D'Or winner and World Player of the Year has scored 27 goals in 82 internationals.

PHILIPP
LAHM

DOB: 11.11.1983

CLUB: Bayern Munich

NATIONALITY: Germany

POSITION: Defence

HEIGHT: 170cm

Few transfer windows go by without Philipp Lahm's name being linked with a big-money transfer. Still only 27, the German captain and full-back, who started life practising against his mum in goal, continues to attract admiring glances from the continent's biggest clubs. He has won three German league and cup doubles in 2006, 2008 and 2010 with Bayern Munich. Able to play on the left or right of defence, Lahm is known not only for his precise tackling but also his attacking ability. He can run at pace, boasts good dribbling skills and has scored a number of stunning goals. He has started every game for his country in the last three major tournaments.

FRANK
LAMPARD

DOB: 20.06.1978

NATIONALITY: England

POSITION: Midfield

HEIGHT: 183cm

CURRENT CLUB:
Chelsea

PREVIOUS CLUBS:
Swansea City (loan),
West Ham United

ENGLAND

Described as the "best box-to-box midfielder in the world" by former Chelsea manager Guus Hiddink, Lampard continues to impress with his consistency, particularly for Chelsea. The three-times winner of the club's Player of the Year award boasts an impressive goalscoring record from midfield (see right). He's the third-highest scorer in Chelsea's history and boasts the Blues' record number of strikes from midfield. His ability to set up others with his incisive passing and peripheral vision make him a dangerous attacking threat. Lampard enjoys a goal every four games for his country, for whom he has 85 caps.

DID YOU KNOW?

Only four midfielders have scored more than 100 goals in the history of the Premier League, which started in 1992. None have scored more than Lampard. He has scored 131, Manchester United's Ryan Giggs has scored 108, Paul Scholes 102, while Southampton legend Matt Le Tissier scored 101.

DIEGO LUGANO

DOB:	02.11.1980
CLUB:	Fenerbahce
NATIONALITY:	Uruguay
POSITION:	Defence
HEIGHT:	188cm

Few defenders stood out at the World Cup in 2010 like Uruguay captain, Diego Lugano. His battling spirit, close marking, aerial ability and commanding presence helped *La Celeste* make it through to the semi-finals. He was crucial in qualifying, too, playing 15 times and scoring three goals. He's not just popular in Uruguay, though; he won every domestic honour during a three-year spell at São Paulo, Brazil, before moving to Turkey in 2006. In his first two seasons at Fenerbahce he was a key performer, winning the league in 2007, reaching the quarter-finals of the Champions League in 2008 and winning the league again in 2011.

MAICON

DOB:	**26.07.1981**
CLUB:	**Inter Milan**
NATIONALITY:	**Brazil**
POSITION:	**Defence**
HEIGHT:	**186cm**

Maicon was among the first of a new wave of attacking full-backs. The Brazilian is a ferocious tackler – on one occasion, against Barcelona, he lost a tooth throwing his body in front of a shot – who has the strength of a central defender. He also has the speed and dribbling skills of a winger, he can deliver an accurate cross and strike at goal. He scored one of the goals of the 2010 World Cup against North Korea. Born in 1981, Maicon made his international debut in 2003 and scored a spectacular goal a year later, against Paraguay, prompting a move to AS Monaco. He left to join Inter Milan in 2006 and in 2009/10 he won the treble.

JAVIER
MASCHERANO

DOB:	**08.06.1984**
CLUB:	**Barcelona**
NATIONALITY:	**Argentina**
POSITION:	**Midfield**
HEIGHT:	**171cm**

In 2009, then Argentina coach Diego Maradona described his team as "Javier Mascherano and 10 others", outlining the defensive midfielder's importance. The San Lorenzo-born 26-year-old is the youngest player to captain his country since Maradona and he is the only Argentinian to have twice won gold at the Olympics. A tireless ball-winner who sits in front of – and protects – his defence, Mascherano was a key player who helped Barcelona win the league, the Champions League and the Spanish Super Cup in his debut season. He left Liverpool in the summer of 2010 and his first campaign in Spain was his most successful season since 2003/04, when he won the Primera Division Clausara with Argentine side River Plate.

FLORENT
MALOUDA

DOB:	13.06.1980
CLUB:	Chelsea
NATIONALITY:	France
POSITION:	Midfield
HEIGHT:	184cm

Powerful winger Florent Malouda describes himself as "the complete player", but he took time to settle at Chelsea following his move from Olympique Lyonnais in 2007. It wasn't until 2009/10 that we began to see the best of the Frenchman. Malouda scored 15 league and cup goals and set up a further 15 before hitting top form at the beginning of the 2010/11 season, when he scored six goals in the opening five games. He has already won one league title since his move to London, but he has some way to go to repeating his success in France. With Olympique Lyonnais, he won four league winner's medals.

LIONEL MESSI

DOB:	24.06.1987
NATIONALITY:	Argentina
POSITION:	Forward
HEIGHT:	170cm

CURRENT CLUB:
Barcelona

PREVIOUS CLUBS:
Newells Old Boys

"Leo is by far the best player in the world," says Barcelona team-mate Xavi, a sentiment concurred by former Argentina coach Diego Maradona, himself considered one of the greatest players of all time and who describes Messi as his "successor". In 2008/09 Messi scored 38 goals – and added 18 assists – as Barca won the treble. He scored 47 in all competitions a year later before smashing his record in a glorious season in 2010/11. He netted 50 goals in all competitions, including 31 in the league and seven in Europe – the highlight his goal in a 3-1 win against Manchester United in the Champions League final at Wembley. It was the fourth time Barca had lifted the trophy, the third piece of silverware of the season for the Argentine.

DID YOU KNOW?

Lionel Messi's trophy cabinet must be the size of a house. He has won 15 club honours, but his list of individual awards is even longer. At the last count, he'd won 63, including occasions when he's been voted into various representative teams. A four-time winner of the Argentina Player of the Year Award he's also won, among other things, the European Footballer of the Year Award and the European Golden Shoe (for most goals scored), in 2009/10.

TOP
50

DIEGO
MILITO

DOB:	12.06.1979
NATIONALITY:	Argentina
POSITION:	Forward
HEIGHT:	177cm

CURRENT CLUB:
Inter Milan

PREVIOUS CLUBS:
Genoa, Real Zaragoza,
Genoa, Racing Club

The Inter Milan and Argentina striker has a delicate touch, great positional sense and powerful finish. In 2009/10 his goals – 30 in 51 games – helped the *Nerazzurri* win the treble. He moved to Italy after leaving first club Racing Club to join Genoa in 2004. He scored 33 goals in 59 matches before joining Real Zaragoza. In his first season he was the club's top scorer with 15 goals, scoring another 23 in 2006/07. He left to rejoin Genoa after bagging 53 goals in 108 games. He scored 24 in 31 in his second spell and subsequently joined Inter.

DID YOU KNOW?

Diego and brother Gabriel have both won the Champions League, Gabriel with Barcelona. They join the Laudrup brothers, the Charltons, Van der Kerkhofs, Nevilles and de Boers as siblings to have played in the European Cup. They played together at Real Zaragoza, in Spain, and in 2010 they faced each other as opponents for the fifth time in their careers. Diego is yet to start a game and win at his brother's expense!

NANI

DOB:	17.11.1986
NATIONALITY:	Portugal
POSITION:	Midfield
HEIGHT:	177cm

CURRENT CLUB:
Manchester United

PREVIOUS CLUBS:
Sporting Lisbon

Portuguese international Nani – who reportedly still sleeps with a football nearby – followed Cristiano Ronaldo from Sporting Lisbon to Manchester United. The Red Devils won a league and European Cup double in his first season, in 2007/08, but it's only since Ronaldo's departure to Real Madrid in 2009 that United fans have seen the best of the Cape Verde-born winger. He started more games, scored a career-high of seven goals and created more from wide positions in 2009/10. The following season he was even more consistent, scoring 10 goals and spinning opposing full-backs in circles.

DID YOU KNOW?

Nani's back flip celebration is inspired by a 'fight dance' called capoeira invented by enslaved Africans in Brazil. The martial art involves two contestants forming a circle in which they try to outwit each other and trip their rival. The practice is danced all over the world, but particularly on Brazilian parks, beaches and streets.

GERARD
PIQUE

DOB:	**02.02.1987**
NATIONALITY:	**Spain**
POSITION:	**Defence**
HEIGHT:	**192cm**

CURRENT CLUB:
Barcelona

PREVIOUS CLUBS:
Manchester United,
Real Zaragoza (loan),
Barcelona

Unable to break the defensive duo of Rio Ferdinand and
Nemanja Vidic at Manchester United, Pique returned to
Barcelona, his first club, in 2007. He left Old Trafford having
won the Champions League and he won it again 12 months later,
aged just 22, with Barcelona, as the Catalan club became the
first Spanish side to win the treble. Barca fans dubbed him 'the
new Beckenbauer' because his height and ease on the ball are
similar to German legend, Franz. He helped Spain win Euro 2008
and the World Cup in 2010 before ending the 2010/11 season
with a trio of medals as Barca completed another treble.

DID YOU KNOW?

Only three other players have joined Pique in winning consecutive Champions League trophies with two different clubs. French defender Marcel Desailly won with Marseille in 1993 and AC Milan in 1994, Portuguese defender Paulo Sousa with Juventus in 1996 and Borussia Dortmund in 1997 and Cameroon striker Samuel Eto'o with Barcelona in 2009 and Inter Milan a year later.

FRANCK
RIBERY

DOB:	07.04.1983
CLUB:	Bayern Munich
NATIONALITY:	France
POSITION:	Midfield
HEIGHT:	175cm

When the Frenchman moved to Bayern Munich from Marseille – the club he supports – in 2007, club president Franz Beckenbauer described the feeling of signing him like "winning the lottery". It's easy to see why. He was voted Bundesliga Player of the Year in his first season, has won two league titles and boasts a goal every three games. His bursts of acceleration, weaving runs and ability to score make him a constant danger. A two-time winner of the French Player of the Year award, he has been described as the 'jewel of French football' by *Les Bleus'* legend, Zinedine Zidane.

ARJEN
ROBBEN

DOB:	**23.01.1984**
CLUB:	**Bayern Munich**
NATIONALITY:	**Holland**
POSITION:	**Midfield**
HEIGHT:	**180cm**

Unstoppable when fit, Dutchman Arjen Robben was one of the most exciting players at the 2010 World Cup in South Africa as Holland reached the final. Left on the bench for the first two games to recover from a hamstring injury, he scored in the second round and again in the semi-final, earning a nomination for Player of the Tournament. This followed a stunning season at Bayern Munich. At his best attacking space on the right and running at defenders, he scored 23 goals in 37 games and lifted the Bundesliga title in 2009/10, his fourth league title in four countries.

CRISTIANO RONALDO

DOB: 05.02.1985

NATIONALITY: Portugal

POSITION: Midfield

HEIGHT: 185cm

CURRENT CLUB:
Real Madrid

PREVIOUS CLUBS:
Manchester United,
Sporting Lisbon,
Nacional

"I am not a god," says Cristiano Ronaldo, but his fans may beg to differ. More than 80,000 supporters packed in to the Bernabeu to greet him when he joined Real Madrid in 2009, beating the 75,000 who greeted Diego Maradona's move from Barcelona to Napoli in 1984. He's already repaid a large portion of his transfer fee (see right) with 33 goals in his first season and 53 in his second, the most amount of goals in one season by a single player in Madrid's history. He scored 84 goals in 196 games for United in total, winning three league titles, one Champions League and an FA Cup.

DID YOU KNOW?

At £80million, the transfer fee Real Madrid paid Manchester United for Ronaldo in 2009 makes him the most expensive player in the world. Zlatan Ibrahimovic, second, cost Barcelona £56.5million, while Kaka cost £56million. Real Madrid were also involved in the fourth-highest transfer fee ever paid. They forked out £35million for attacking midfielder Zinedine Zidane, who joined from Juventus, in 2001.

WAYNE
ROONEY

DOB: 24.10.1985

NATIONALITY: England

POSITION: Forward

HEIGHT: 178cm

CURRENT CLUB:
Manchester United

PREVIOUS CLUBS:
Everton

ENGLAND

In 2009/10 Rooney improved his already-impressive positioning, heading and link-up play and top-scored for his country in World Cup qualifying with nine goals. For Manchester United, in the absence of Cristiano Ronaldo who joined Real Madrid in 2009, he scored 34 goals in all competitions. This followed 20 in 49 games the previous season, which culminated in his third league title since joining United from Everton in 2004. In 2010/11 Rooney bounced back to his best after several absences through injury. He had a disappointing World Cup and slow start to 2010/11, but returned to form with an incredible overhead kick against Manchester City before winning his fourth league title with United.

DID YOU KNOW?

Wayne Rooney is a huge boxing fan. He gave up the sport at a young age to pursue his football career, but even now he spars in an effort to keep fit and he's a regular at major bouts. He's strong, too: he once beat Ricky Hatton, former WBA Welterweight Champion, in an arm-wrestling match.

BASTIAN
SCHWEINSTEIGER

DOB: 01.08.1984

CLUB: Bayern Munich

NATIONALITY: Germany

POSITION: Midfield

HEIGHT: 180cm

Technically-gifted, Schweinsteiger can play on either flank but feels "more comfortable" in front of the back four playing as a defensive midfielder. However, his balance (attributed to his skiing ability as a child), potential to shoot from distance and ability to use both feet means he is becoming more of a playmaker. Still only 26, Schweinsteiger boasts a staggering 83 international caps. He is one of Bayern Munich's longest-serving players after signing aged 14 in 1998. Since then he has won five Bundesliga titles, five German cups and two league cups.

WESLEY SNEIJDER

TOP 50

DOB:	09.06.1984
CLUB:	Inter Milan
NATIONALITY:	Holland
POSITION:	Midfield
HEIGHT:	170cm

KNVB

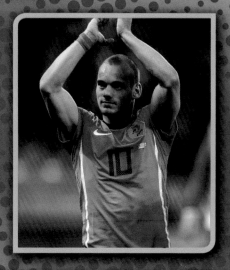

If 2008/09 represented a difficult season for attacking midfielder Wesley Sneijder, 2009/10 made up for it. The Dutchman was injured in his last campaign for Real Madrid, for whom he'd won the league title in his first season. Yet after joining Inter Milan, Sneijder returned to his best and helped the *Nerazzurri* win the treble. In South Africa in 2010, he was instrumental as Holland reached the World Cup final. They were beaten by Spain, but Sneijder's passing, shooting from set pieces and ability to score from range made him one of the players of the tournament. The 2010/11 season was only the second in his professional career in which he has failed to win a trophy.

JOHN TERRY

DOB:	**07.12.1980**
NATIONALITY:	**England**
POSITION:	**Defender**
HEIGHT:	**188cm**

CURRENT CLUB:
Chelsea

PREVIOUS CLUBS:
Nottingham Forest
(loan), West Ham United

ENGLAND

Chelsea captain John Terry is known best for his strong tackles, fearless leadership and excellent heading ability. He has been at the London club since he was 14. He makes well-timed challenges while his will-to-win and ability to make his presence felt at both ends of the pitch make him an important player for club and country. He's as capable scoring a crucial goal as making a last-ditch tackle. He's also an excellent passer of the ball. Terry is believed to have around 50 match rituals that include wearing lucky shin pads. He has won three league titles and four FA Cups as Chelsea captain.

DID YOU KNOW?

On 1 June 2007, John Terry became the first player to score for – and captain – the senior England team at the new Wembley Stadium when he scored England's first goal in a 1–1 draw during a friendly against Brazil. He scored from a header following a cross from a free-kick by David Beckham. "It's going to live with me forever," he said. This feat came just 13 days after Terry became the first player to lift the FA Cup at the new stadium following Chelsea's 1-0 win against Manchester United.

CARLOS
TEVEZ

DOB:	05.02.1984
CLUB:	Manchester City
NATIONALITY:	Argentina
POSITION:	Forward
HEIGHT:	173cm

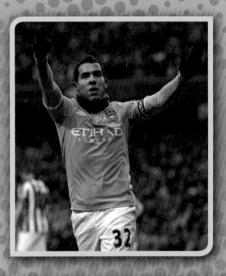

For someone who repeatedly says he doesn't enjoy playing football and could walk away from the game, Argentine international Carlos Tevez is one of the world's best strikers. He scored nine goals in his first seven games in 2010/11 – 21 in total – while his ability to inspire his team-mates with goals and a never-say-die attitude prompted Manchester City boss Roberto Mancini to give him the captain's armband. After winning two league titles and a European Cup in two seasons with Manchester United he became the first player to leave for cross-city rivals City since Terry Cooke in 1999. Won the FA Cup in his first season at Eastlands.

FERNANDO TORRES

DOB:	20.03.1984
CLUB:	Chelsea
NATIONALITY:	Spain
POSITION:	Forward
HEIGHT:	181cm

The Spanish striker had a frustrating year in 2010, but he remains one of the world's best strikers. Injuries prevented him from hitting top gear at the World Cup and in the opening months of the Premier League season, but previously 'El Nino' had been a big hit at Liverpool. His explosive pace, lethal finishing and aerial ability culminated in 50 goals in his first 84 games, 34 coming in his first season. He also scored the club's 1,000th Premier League goal. This followed 84 goals in 214 games for his hometown club, Atletico Madrid. In January 2011 he joined Chelsea in a deal worth £50million, making him the fifth most expensive footballer in the world.

YAYA TOURE

DOB:	13.05.1983
CLUB:	Manchester City
NATIONALITY:	Ivory Coast
POSITION:	Midfield
HEIGHT:	189cm

A powerful midfield player who can also play in defence, Yaya Toure scored the goal that won the FA Cup in his first season at Manchester City after joining from Barcelona in 2010. He won a La Liga and Champions League double in his last season at the Nou Camp, his second successive league triumph with the Catalan club, before joining brother Kolo in Manchester. The Ivory Coast international has not only become one of the highest paid footballers in the English league following his £24million move, he has also helped City finish in the top four and qualify for the Champions League with a string of impressive performances.

ROBIN
VAN PERSIE

DOB:	**06.08.1983**
CLUB:	**Arsenal**
NATIONALITY:	**Holland**
POSITION:	**Forward**
HEIGHT:	**184cm**

Injuries have hampered the Dutch striker's career, but he continues to be a major source of goals for club and country when fit to play. Van Persie netted his 19th goal in 51 internationals en route to Holland reaching the World Cup final in 2010. He joined Arsenal from Feyenoord – where he spent three seasons and lifted the UEFA Cup in 2002 – in 2004 and lifted the FA Community Shield and FA Cup in his first season. Van Persie has failed to add to his trophy cabinet since, despite scoring more than a goal every three games in club colours. He'll be hoping the Gunners can rectify this record in 2012.

NEMANJA
VIDIC

DOB:	21.10.1981
CLUB:	Manchester United
NATIONALITY:	Serbia
POSITION:	Defence
HEIGHT:	185cm

Fearless in the tackle and formidable in the air, Nemanja Vidic is hailed by club manager Sir Alex Ferguson as the best defender in the world. Current captain for Manchester United and Serbia, he has won four Premier League titles, three League Cups, three Community Shields, the Champions League and Club World Cup – all since joining United in 2006. In 2008/09 he was named Premier League Player of the Year after featuring in United's record run of 14 consecutive clean sheets. He made his international debut in 2002 and helped Serbia keep four clean sheets in qualifying for the World Cup in 2010.

DOB:	03.12.1981
CLUB:	Barcelona
NATIONALITY:	Spain
POSITION:	Forward
HEIGHT:	175cm

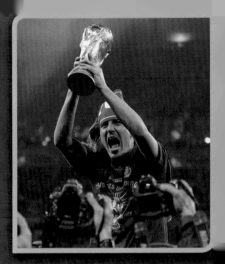

After lifting the World Cup in 2010, David Villa took his remarkable scoring record and incisive runs from Valencia to Barcelona, boasting a record of 140 goals in 239 La Liga games. In South Africa he became the most-prolific Spaniard in World Cup history, scoring four to add to the three he bagged in 2006. In October 2010, he surpassed Raul's record of 44 goals to become the country's all-time top goalscorer. He won the Golden Boot at Euro 2008 as Spain won the competition for the first time in 44 years and in 2009 he became the first Spaniard to score in six consecutive international matches.

XAVI

DOB:	**25.01.1980**
NATIONALITY:	**Spain**
POSITION:	**Midfield**
HEIGHT:	**170cm**

CURRENT CLUB:
Barcelona

PREVIOUS CLUBS:
n/a

Xavi pulls the strings for club and country and has won every trophy at both levels. Even as early as 1999, when he captained Spain's Under-20 team, he lifted the World Cup. Eleven years later he won the real thing in South Africa. Between the two he won the European Championship in 2008 – when he was voted Player of the tournament – and has also won six league titles, one Spanish Cup, five Spanish Supercups and one Club World Cup at domestic level. A one-club man now approaching 400 appearances for Barcelona, Xavi has also added three Champions League winners' medals – 2006, 2009 and 2011 – to his collection of silverware.

DID YOU KNOW?

Xavi is considered the best midfielder on the planet and the statistics prove it. In the World Cup in 2010 he made more passes, more successful passes and more balls into the penalty area than any other player. In the Champions League final in 2011 he covered the most ground and made 148 passes – of which 95 per cent were successful – which is more than any player in a single game in the competition in 2010/11.

NEW TO YOU

The World Cup in South Africa produced a number of new stars while the 2010/11 season saw new talents emerge on the world stage

SERGIO AGUERO	74	ANGEL DI MARIA	90
ANTHONY ANNAN	75	JUAN MATA	91
GARETH BALE	76	THOMAS MÜLLER	92
MARIO BALOTELLI	77	IKER MUNIAIN	93
SERGIO CANALES	78	SAMIR NASRI	94
FÁBIO COENTRÃO	79	MESUT OZIL	95
DOUGLAS COSTA	80	ALEXANDRE PATO	96
PHILIPPE COUTINHO	81	MIRALEM PJANIC	97
STEVEN DEFOUR	82	RAMIRES	98
YOANN GOURCUFF	83	PEDRO RODRIGUEZ	99
JOE HART	84	JACK RODWELL	100
JAVIER HERNANDEZ	85	DAVIDE SANTON	101
LEWIS HOLTBY	86	DAVID SILVA	102
GONZALO HIGUAIN	87	CHRIS SMALLING	103
SAMI KHEDIRA	88	THEO WALCOTT	104
ADAM JOHNSON	89	JACK WILSHERE	105

SERGIO AGUERO

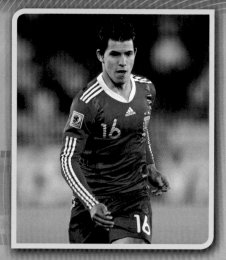

DOB:	02.06.1988
CLUB:	Atletico Madrid
NATIONALITY:	Argentina
POSITION:	Forward
HEIGHT:	170cm

Young Argentine striker Aguero already has four years of international experience and the 2010/11 season was his eighth since turning professional. He was Argentina's joint-top scorer with four in qualifying for the World Cup in 2010, while his ability to take on defenders and cool finishing have made him a fans' favourite at Atletico Madrid. He joined *Los Colchoneros* in 2006 from Independiente, for whom he became the youngest player in the Argentine First Division aged 15 years and 35 days in 2003. In 2007/08 he scored 20 goals and helped his side qualify for the Champions League.

ANTHONY ANNAN

DOB:	21.07.1986
CLUB:	Schalke
NATIONALITY:	Ghana
POSITION:	Midfield
HEIGHT:	171cm

Ghana's next major football star, 24-year-old Annan already has more than 40 caps for the Black Stars after making his debut in 2007. His commanding and assured performances at the World Cup in South Africa in 2010 have seen him become a target for Europe's biggest clubs. He currently plays for Norwegian side Rosenborg, for whom he helped win the league title in 2009. It was Annan's second Tippeligaen title having helped Stabaek clinch the league title while on loan in 2008. A talented midfield player, he is also strong in the tackle.

GARETH
BALE

NEW TO YOU

DOB:	16.07.1989
CLUB:	Tottenham Hotspur
NATIONALITY:	Wales
POSITION:	Defence
HEIGHT:	183cm

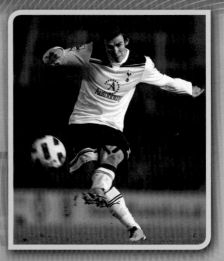

A powerful and quick left-sided player who can perform in defence or midfield, Bale set an unwanted record of 24 games without being on the winning side in his first two years after joining Tottenham Hotspur, in 2007. However, the Welsh international turned it around as the North London side qualified for the Champions League in 2009/10 and his electrifying form continued in 2010/11. He scored twice and set up four goals in two games in the space of four days in August before hitting an incredible hat-trick against Inter Milan at the San Siro in October. He won the PFA Player of the Year Award at the end of the season.

MARIO BALOTELLI

DOB: 12.08.1990

CLUB: Manchester City

NATIONALITY: Italy

POSITION: Forward

HEIGHT: 189cm

With a quick turn of pace, the ability to score goals from close range or from distance and play anywhere along the leading line, the player described as "the first black superstar of Italian football" made his full international debut in 2010, against the Ivory Coast. He joined Manchester City in the summer of 2010 for £24million. Balotelli rejoined his former boss Roberto Mancini, who gave the striker his first start at Inter Milan in 2007. He won three titles in three seasons at the San Siro, but never seemed to be too far from controversy, on or off the field.

SERGIO
CANALES

DOB: 16.02.1991

CLUB: Real Madrid

NATIONALITY: Spain

POSITION: Forward

HEIGHT: 176cm

Eyebrows were raised when Real Madrid signed left-footed attacking midfielder Canales from Racing Santander for around £4million, but he has already broken into Madrid's first team. Perhaps helped by the long-term injury to Brazilian international Kaka, Canales has shown glimpses of his potential when selected. In his final season at Santander, his hometown club and where he climbed the club's ranks, he scored six goals and made four assists. He also scored two goals in his first two U21 internationals having already won a European Championship at U17 level in 2008.

FÁBIO
COENTRÃO

DOB:	**11.03.1988**
CLUB:	**Benfica**
NATIONALITY:	**Portugal**
POSITION:	**Defence**
HEIGHT:	**179cm**

A winner of the Portuguese League's Breakthrough Player of the Year award while at Rio Ave in 2006/07, Coentrão had already enjoyed a successful season with Benfica before his performances at the World Cup projected his talents onto a bigger stage. He started every game before Portugal were knocked out in the last 16 by Spain, but his ability to get forward and take players on from a defensive position saw him emerge as one of the stars of the tournament. This followed 43 games as his club side won a League and League Cup double in 2009/10.

DOUGLAS
COSTA

DOB: 14.09.1990

CLUB: FC Shakhtar Donetsk

NATIONALITY: Brazil

POSITION: Midfield

HEIGHT: 170cm

A left-footed attacking midfielder who can play on the flanks, Brazilian Costa boasts great ability, good vision and has a knack of scoring spectacular goals from free-kicks. He currently plays in Ukraine for Shakhtar Donetsk, who he joined from Gremio in 2009. He scored on his debut for the Brazilian side and was soon dubbed 'the new Ronaldinho', largely because of his trickery. He had to wait for his chance at Donetsk, although his side won the league title in his first season. In 2010/11, his second season, he scored five from his first 12 appearances.

PHILIPPE COUTINHO

DOB:	**12.06.1992**
CLUB:	**Inter Milan**
NATIONALITY:	**Brazil**
POSITION:	**Midfield**
HEIGHT:	**171cm**

Described as "the future of Inter" by former manager Rafael Benitez, Coutinho is an exciting Brazilian talent who can use both feet and beat opposing players with a combination of skills and tricks. He scored his first Inter goal, a stunning volley, in a pre-season friendly against Panathinaikos in the summer of 2010, and while he is still feeling his way in Serie A, he is considered one of the brightest talents in the division. He joined the *Nerazzurri* from Brazilian side Vasco da Gama and was initially loaned back to gain first-team experience.

STEVEN DEFOUR

DOB:	15.04.1988
CLUB:	Standard Liege
NATIONALITY:	Belgium
POSITION:	Midfield
HEIGHT:	174cm

Twenty-three year old midfielder Steven Defour continues to attract admiring glances from Europe's biggest clubs with his midfield play. He made his debut for Racing Genk at the age of 16 and made 30 appearances for the club before Standard Liege snapped him up. Defour was made Liege captain at 19 and at the end of the season he was awarded the Golden Shoe for being the most valuable player in Belgium. In 2008/09, he led his side to their first Jupiter League title in 25 years and – after repeating his success in 2009/10 – rumours of a move abroad continue to spread.

YOANN GOURCUFF

DOB: 11.07.1986
CLUB: Olympique Lyonnais
NATIONALITY: France
POSITION: Midfield
HEIGHT: 185cm

Yoann Gourcuff is the latest player to be described as 'the next Zinedine Zidane' while former French international David Ginola believes he's the "best player of his generation". He's already made more than 25 appearances for *Les Bleus* in two years and in 2008/09 he scored 12 goals and contributed 10 assists as he helped Bordeaux win the French league title. He was named French Player of the Year and in 2010 he joined rivals Olympique Lyonnais. In his early career he was a fans' favourite at Rennes. He spent three seasons with the French side before joining AC Milan, and later Bordeaux.

JOE HART

DOB: 19.04.1987
CLUB: Manchester City
NATIONALITY: England
POSITION: Goalkeeper
HEIGHT: 191cm

ENGLAND

After a successful 2009/10 season on loan at Birmingham City, Hart forced his way into the no.1 slot at Manchester City at the expense of experienced goalkeeper, Shay Given. Hart has also become Fabio Capello's first choice for England as a result of his shot-stopping ability, quick reflexes and smart decision-making. As a youngster he was Shrewsbury Town's no.1 before the age of 18 and played well enough to join up with England's U19 team. He moved up to the U21s and joined current club City, from where he also had successful loan spells at Tranmere Rovers and Blackpool.

JAVIER
HERNANDEZ

DOB: 01.06.1988

CLUB: Manchester United

NATIONALITY: Mexico

POSITION: Forward

HEIGHT: 175cm

If people were surprised by Sir Alex Ferguson's decision to sign little known Mexican Javier Hernandez before the World Cup, then the youngster's performances in South Africa and in 2010/11 have justified it. 'Chicharito' or 'Little Pea' – whose father and grandfather both represented Mexico – scored twice during the tournament and at 19.98mph, he was timed as the World Cup's quickest player. He has scored 14 goals in 23 internationals to date. Dangerous with his head despite his small size, Hernandez is quick, intelligent and boasts a remarkable shooting ability. He scored on his competitive United debut and finished his first season in England with 20 goals.

LEWIS
HOLTBY

DOB:	18.09.1990
CLUB:	Schalke
NATIONALITY:	Germany
POSITION:	Midfield
HEIGHT:	174cm

Few England fans had heard of Lewis Holtby before 2010, but his rise to prominence coincided with loan side FC Mainz's impressive start to the 2010/11 season. The German side won their opening five games to challenge at the top of the Bundesliga. The attacking midfielder, who reckons he "plays like Joe Cole" has been key to the club's surprise success, but he has also starred at various levels for Germany, from the U18s and U20s, culminating in the captaincy of the U21 side. Born to an English father and a German mother, he has declared he wants to play for Germany.

GONZALO
HIGUAIN

DOB: 10.12.1987
CLUB: Real Madrid
NATIONALITY: Argentina
POSITION: Forward
HEIGHT: 184cm

The third Argentine international to score a World Cup hat-trick, against South Korea in 2010, Higuain has had to be patient at club level. He joined Real Madrid from River Plate in January 2007 but was kept out of the side by more experienced strikers. A series of crucial goals – starting a title charge in 2007, another securing the league title a year later – afforded him more opportunities and in 2008/09 he top-scored with 22. Despite Real buying Kaka, Cristiano Ronaldo and Karim Benzema in 2009/10, only Lionel Messi scored more in La Liga than Higuain. He is fast, intelligent and can run with the ball.

SAMI KHEDIRA

DOB: 04.04.1987
CLUB: Real Madrid
NATIONALITY: Germany
POSITION: Midfield
HEIGHT: 189cm

A fringe player for Germany until the World Cup in 2010, holding-midfielder Sami Khedira showed the world what Stuttgart fans already knew, he's one of the best in the business. He can link defence with attack and dictate a match. His incisive passing can create attacking opportunities while his ability to read the game – coupled with his aerial presence – make him a strong barrier in front of the defence. The 24-year-old was at Stuttgart from the age of eight. In his first season with the senior team, 2006/07, he played a key role as they won the Bundesliga. He joined Real Madrid in 2010.

ADAM JOHNSON

DOB: 14.07.1987
CLUB: Manchester City
NATIONALITY: England
POSITION: Midfield
HEIGHT: 180cm

ENGLAND

Adam Johnson's performances for club and country at the start of the 2010/11 season were sensational. He scored his first England goal in only his second start, against Bulgaria in a European Championship qualifier. He scored another against Switzerland and impressed against Montenegro, when his pace, willingness to take on defenders and have a shot made him difficult to defend against. Competition for places at big spenders Manchester City mean Johnson isn't guaranteed a starting place, but he scored key goals in 2010/11 and his ability to switch from one flank to the other gives him an advantage.

ANGEL
DI MARIA

DOB: 14.02.1988
CLUB: Real Madrid
NATIONALITY: Argentina
POSITION: Midfield
HEIGHT: 178cm

Angel di Maria is a technically-gifted winger with bags of pace, who impressed at the World Cup in 2010 before joining Real Madrid from Benfica. The Argentinian played all five games in South Africa and proved a constant menace on the left-flank, this after winning a league and league cup double in Portugal in 2009/10. He can create goals as well as score them and he's had no problems finding the net for his new club. He scored three times in pre-season and took just three games to open his La Liga account.

JUAN
MATA

NEW TO YOU

DOB:	28.04.1988
CLUB:	Valencia
NATIONALITY:	Spain
POSITION:	Midfield
HEIGHT:	170cm

The small, lightning-fast Valencia playmaker is revelling as star man following the departure of former team-mate David Villa to Barcelona in 2010. Mata helped fire his team-mates to La Liga's top spot temporarily with one goal and three assists. He scored five goals in 24 matches in his first season, in 2007/08, and followed that with 11 in 37 a year later. A striker by trade, he plays in an advanced left-winger position where his cool finishing skills are reminiscent of his hero, Brazilian striker Romario. Made his international debut in the Confederations Cup in 2009.

THOMAS MÜLLER

DOB:	13.09.1989
CLUB:	Bayern Munich
NATIONALITY:	Germany
POSITION:	Midfield
HEIGHT:	186cm

"I like to keep it simple," said Müller before the World Cup in South Africa. His style proved effective. He was given the no.13 shirt as previously worn by Michael Ballack and seized his chance in the centre of the midfield, emerging as one of the biggest stars of the tournament. He scored five goals in six appearances, provided three assists and not only picked up the Golden Boot, but was also named Best Young Player. This followed a fine first full season as a professional. He scored 19 goals in 52 games for Bayern Munich and was named in the Bundesliga team of the year.

IKER
MUNIAIN

NEW TO YOU

DOB:	19.12.1992
CLUB:	Atletico Madrid
NATIONALITY:	Spain
POSITION:	Forward
HEIGHT:	168cm

The 2009/10 season was Muniain's first in professional football. He became the youngest player in Atletico Bilbao history when he came on as a substitute in July aged just 16 days and seven months. One week later he played, and found the net, making him the club's youngest scorer in history. In August 2010, he started his first league match and became the youngest *Los Leones* player to feature in La Liga, scoring his first goal in October. He has been described as having a similar style to Lionel Messi with his close ball control, low centre of gravity and ability to unlock defences.

SAMIR
NASRI

DOB:	26.06.1987
CLUB:	Arsenal
NATIONALITY:	France
POSITION:	Midfield
HEIGHT:	180cm

A clever player who can operate in the centre of midfield or on either wing, Nasri scored four goals at Euro 2008 and despite missing out on selection for the World Cup in 2010, he has featured in France's midfield since, playing in the centre alongside Yoann Gourcuff. Nasri scored 16 goals in 41 appearances in the 2010/11 season for Arsenal and is becoming one of the most consistent performers in the Premier League. He's best known for his vision and close dribbling skills. In 2007, while at Marseille, he was voted Player of the Year in Ligue 1.

MESUT ÖZIL

DOB:	**15.10.1988**
CLUB:	**Real Madrid**
NATIONALITY:	**Germany**
POSITION:	**Midfield**
HEIGHT:	**180cm**

"Özil is a gift for German football," said national coach Joachim Löw as he watched the Turkish-born playmaker lead the U21s to European Championship glory in 2009 and the senior side to the quarter-finals of the World Cup 12 months later. Özil can play on the wing or just off the strikers and his dazzling displays in South Africa saw him nominated as player of the tournament. Ozil left boyhood club Schalke for Werder Bremen in January 2008 and seamlessly filled the boots vacated by Brazilian playmaker Diego, leading the side to German Cup glory in 2009. He joined Real Madrid in 2010.

ALEXANDRE
PATO

DOB:	02.09.1989
CLUB:	AC Milan
NATIONALITY:	Brazil
POSITION:	Forward
HEIGHT:	179cm

Brazilian striker Alexandre Pato, who survived a tumour as a child, took just one minute to score on his professional debut, for Internacional in November 2006. He hit the bar, set up two more before he was substituted in the 58th-minute and given a standing ovation. He joined AC Milan in 2007 and again netted on his debut, against Napoli. He started 2010/11 with four goals in four games and ended the campaign with 14 League goals as Milan won the Serie A title. He enjoyed further debut joy by netting the only goal in Brazil's 1-0 win over Sweden during his first international start, in March 2008.

MIRALEM PJANIC

NEW TO YOU

DOB: 02.04.1990

CLUB: Olympique Lyonnais

NATIONALITY: Bosnia & Herzegovina

POSITION: Midfield

HEIGHT: 180cm

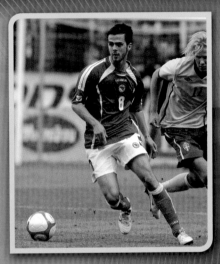

Olympique Lyonnais' loss of playmaker and free-kick specialist Juninho Pernambucano to Qatar club Al-Gharafa was Miralem Pjanic's gain. The Bosnian midfielder seized the Brazilian's no.8 shirt in his second season after joining from relegated Metz in 2008 and quickly assumed his midfield responsibilities, becoming the club's main source of creativity from open play and set pieces. He was particularly impressive as Olympique Lyonnais reached the semi-finals of the Champions League in 2009/10. He made his international debut in August 2008 in a friendly against Bulgaria and helped Bosnia reach the 2010 World Cup play-offs, only to be beaten by Portugal.

RAMIRES

DOB:	24.03.1989
CLUB:	Chelsea
NATIONALITY:	Brazil
POSITION:	Midfield
HEIGHT:	179cm

Before the World Cup in 2010, midfielder Ramires had won 12 of the 14 matches he played for Brazil. Without him, *A Selecao* lost the 2008 Olympic semi-final in Beijing. His record continued in South Africa. Brazil won three of the four matches he played, drew the other before he missed out on the quarter-final defeat against Holland. His impressive rise to prominence coincided with a move from Brazilians Cruzeiro to Portuguese side Benfica, for whom he won the league title in his first season. He joined Chelsea in 2010, where former boss Carlo Ancelotti hailed him as the future of the club.

PEDRO
RODRIGUEZ

DOB:	**28.07.1987**
CLUB:	**Barcelona**
NATIONALITY:	**Spain**
POSITION:	**Midfield**
HEIGHT:	**169cm**

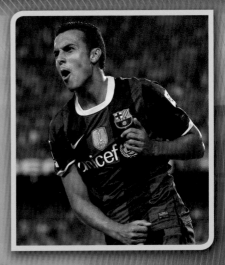

Pedro Rodriguez joined Barcelona aged 17 and made his first team debut in January 2008. At the end of the 2008/09 season the winger claimed he had "won the lottery" when he came on as a substitute in the Champions League final. In 2009/10, he scored 23 goals in 31 starts and was the first player to score in six club competitions in a single season – finding the net in La Liga, Champions League, Super Cup, Copa del Rey, Spanish Super Cup, and World Club Cup. He won a World Cup winners' medal in 2010 and a treble at club level a year later.

JACK
RODWELL

DOB:	11.03.1991
CLUB:	Everton
NATIONALITY:	England
POSITION:	Midfield
HEIGHT:	179cm

ENGLAND

England fans have high hopes for defensive-midfielder Jack Rodwell. He has represented the *Three Lions* at U16, U17, U19 and U21 levels with distinction, particularly impressing at the U21 European Championship in Sweden in 2009. Many believe it won't be long before he's given the chance to impress for the senior side. Born in Southport, he made his Everton debut in March 2008 and has already made more than 50 appearances for the Toffees. He can play in the centre of defence, but it's his athleticism, comfort on the ball and persistence in a deep-lying midfield anchor role that have impressed most.

DAVIDE SANTON

DOB:	02.01.1991
CLUB:	Inter Milan
NATIONALITY:	Italy
POSITION:	Defence
HEIGHT:	187cm

An exciting left-back, Italian fans are hoping Santon can fill the gap left by legend Paolo Maldini, who recently retired. The early signs are promising. He made his full debut for Inter Milan against Roma in the Coppa Italia in January 2009 and excelled against Manchester United later that year, when he performed well against Cristiano Ronaldo. "I was impressed," said the Portuguese winger of his young opponent. "He is a great footballer." The full-back won the Scudetto, the Italian league title, in 2008/09 and earned his first full cap in June 2009, prompting *Azzurri* boss Marcello Lippi to describe him as the "pre-destined one".

DAVID SILVA

DOB: 08.01.1986

CLUB: Manchester City

NATIONALITY: Spain

POSITION: Midfield

HEIGHT: 170cm

David Silva has been a key player for Manchester City since joining from Valencia in June 2010. The small and skilful attacking midfielder has the ability to play on the wing, or behind the strikers and he is known as much for his assists than his goals. City team-mate Carlos Tevez suggests Silva is: "The best signing we have made. He is the type of player who can win you a game." The Spanish international was a fringe player in the squads that won both the European Championship in 2008 and World Cup in 2010. He won the Copa Del Rey with Valencia in 2008 and the FA Cup in 2011 to cap a fine first season at City.

CHRIS
SMALLING

DOB:	**22.11.1989**
CLUB:	**Manchester United**
NATIONALITY:	**England**
POSITION:	**Defence**
HEIGHT:	**192cm**

ENGLAND

Chris Smalling completed a meteoric rise from one MUFC to another when he joined Manchester United in the summer of 2010. The defender started his career at non-league Maidstone United before joining Fulham in 2008. He made his first team debut for the Cottagers during the last game of the 2008/09 season and continued to impress in 2009/10. He made his England U21 debut in August 2009 and would later score his first goal for the Three lions in October 2010. By then, Sir Alex Ferguson had made Smalling a Manchester United player and he has impressed at both Premier League and European level.

THEO
WALCOTT

DOB:	16.03.1989
CLUB:	Arsenal
NATIONALITY:	England
POSITION:	Forward
HEIGHT:	170cm

ENGLAND

Quick, versatile and increasingly prolific in front of goal, Walcott is delivering on the promise he displayed as a young player. Of course, his landmark moment was a hat-trick for England against Croatia in September, 2008, but now it looks as if he will become a more consistent performer for Arsenal. He bagged the first hat-trick of his club career, against Blackpool in August 2010, and added strikes against Blackburn Rovers and Newcastle United. "Before he rushed his decision, but now he is different," says Gunners boss Arsene Wenger. "He is very close to playing that striker role," he continued, a transition enjoyed by Thierry Henry.

JACK
WILSHERE

DOB:	**01.01.1992**
CLUB:	**Arsenal**
NATIONALITY:	**England**
POSITION:	**Midfield**
HEIGHT:	**170cm**

ENGLAND

So far, 2011 has been a huge year for Jack Wilshere. Not just a regular in the Arsenal side but one of the most impressive performers, Wilshere has excelled protecting the back four while passing the ball with confidence in midfield. He has also enjoyed a growing presence in the England team, with Three Lions Coach Fabio Capello describing him as "incredible for someone so young," following a win against Denmark in February 2011. Despite his size, he's tough in the tackle and his creativity going forward – his dribbling ability and movement able to penetrate opposing defences – make him one of England's most exciting rising stars.

LEGENDS

These 20 stars are among the most experienced in the game and in 2010/11 they were still going strong.

MICHAEL BALLACK	108	ANDREA PIRLO	118
GIANLUIGI BUFFON	109	CARLES PUYOL	119
ESTEBAN CAMBIASSO	110	RAUL	120
RICARDO CARVALHO	111	RONALDO	121
JÚLIO CÉSAR	112	RONALDINHO	122
ALESSANDRO DEL PIERO	113	MARCOS SENNA	123
RYAN GIGGS	114	PAUL SCHOLES	124
MIROSLAV KLOSE	115	FRANCESCO TOTTI	125
LUCIO	116	EDWIN VAN DER SAR	126
RUUD VAN NISTELROOY	117	JAVIER ZANETTI	127

MICHAEL BALLACK

DOB: 26.09.1976

NATIONALITY: Germany

POSITION: Midfield

CURRENT CLUB:
Bayer Leverkusen

PREVIOUS CLUBS:
Chelsea, Bayern Munich,
Bayer Leverkusen,
FC Kaiserslautern,
Chemnitzer

A tackle from Portsmouth's Kevin-Prince Boateng in the 2010 FA Cup final prevented Ballack from playing in the World Cup that year, while a subsequent injury kept him out of action until 2011 following his summer move to Bayer Leverkusen from Chelsea. However, Ballack remains Germany's first-choice captain and the national side have not lost a game in which he's scored since June 2005. The midfielder has finished runner-up at both the European Championship and World Cup, but he has won the double in England and Germany. Twice a beaten finalist, only the Champions League has eluded the powerful midfielder.

GIANLUIGI BUFFON

DOB: 28.01.1978

NATIONALITY: Italy

POSITION: Goalkeeper

CURRENT CLUB:
Juventus

PREVIOUS CLUBS:
Parma

Gianluigi Buffon is one of the most successful Italian goalkeepers of all time, and he's still going. A World Cup winner in 2006, when his penalty save at the expense of David Trezeguet ensured victory against France, he has also been named world goalkeeper of the year four times and Serie A's best stopper on seven occasions. He has also lifted the UEFA Cup, the Coppa Italia, Serie A and the Supercoppa Italiania. Still at Juventus after joining from Parma in 2001, the 2010/11 campaign was his 10th season with the *Bianconeri*.

ESTEBAN CAMBIASSO

LEGEND

DOB: 18.08.1980

NATIONALITY: Argentina

POSITION: Midfield

CURRENT CLUB:
Inter Milan

PREVIOUS CLUBS:
Real Madrid, River Plate, Independiente

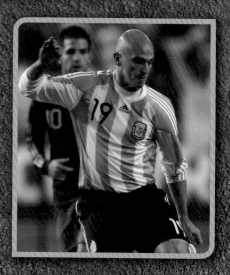

Argentine defensive midfielder Esteban Cambiasso passed 200 Serie A appearances for Inter Milan in 2011 after joining the club in 2004. A crucial part of the team, the highlight of his stay at the Giuseppe Meazza Stadium is the club's historic Scudetto, Coppa Italia and Champions League treble in 2009/10. He has played for the Argentina national team for 10 years, notably putting the finishing touch to a famous 24-pass move against Serbia & Montenegro during the 2006 World Cup. Despite being left out of their squad four years later, Cambiasso returned to the fold in August 2010 and was expected to reach – and surpass – 50 caps in 2011.

RICARDO
CARVALHO

LEGEND

DOB: 18.05.1978

NATIONALITY: Portugal

POSITION: Defence

CURRENT CLUB:
Real Madrid

PREVIOUS CLUBS:
Chelsea, Alverca (loan),
Vitoria de Setubal (loan),
Leca (loan), FC Porto

Ricardo Carvalho has played at the top level ever since he broke into the FC Porto side in 2001 and the centre-back continues to impress at new club Real Madrid, where he became one of new coach Jose Mourinho's first signings in 2010. The Spanish giants will be hoping the quick Portuguese international can bring the success he enjoyed at previous clubs. He helped Madrid lift the Copa del Rey in 2011, but in Portugal he won two league titles, the UEFA Cup and Champions League, all under Mourinho, who took him to Chelsea in 2004. He won a further six trophies in six years in London.

JÚLIO CÉSAR

DOB: 03.09.1979

NATIONALITY: Brazil

POSITION: Goalkeeper

CURRENT CLUB:
Inter Milan

PREVIOUS CLUBS:
Chievo, Flamengo

He may not have added World Cup glory to the treble he won with Inter in 2010, but Cesar was ever-present in goal for Brazil in South Africa, just as he was when they won the Confederations Cup in 2009. A commanding shot-stopper who's always alert, he has won a long list of honours including four Serie A titles and, in 2009, the Italian division's goalkeeper of the Year award. He made his international debut in 2004 and became a regular at Inter a year later. He remains no.1 for club and country.

ALESSANDRO
DEL PIERO

DOB: 09.11.1974

NATIONALITY: Italy

POSITION: Forward

CURRENT CLUB:
Juventus

PREVIOUS CLUBS:
Padova

Diego Maradona once suggested Del Piero "never grows old". The Argentine legend could be right, for while the Italian striker is 36, the Juventus captain scored his 200th Serie A goal for the *Bianconeri* in November 2010. Although he hasn't represented the national team since September 2008, Del Piero has declared he's always available and will play on until he's 40, if selected. He's one of five players to have won 90 or more Italian caps and he's the *Azzurri*'s fourth all-time leading scorer with 27 goals. The playmaker has been at Juve since 1993, even remaining loyal to the club when they were demoted in 2006

RYAN GIGGS

DOB: 29.11.1973

NATIONALITY: Wales

POSITION: Midfield

CURRENT CLUB:
Manchester United

PREVIOUS CLUBS:
n/a

Ryan Giggs' goal against Newcastle United in the 2010/11 season continued his record of scoring in every campaign since the inception of the Premier League in 1992. In 2009 he broke Sir Bobby Charlton's record of most appearances for Manchester United and in the same year he became the first player to win 11 Premier League titles. In 2011 he won his 12th. For many years he played as a winger, but Giggs now fills more of a holding role in the centre of midfield. His ability to read the game but dribble with elegance continues to amaze his manager and fans. The Welshman was awarded an OBE for services to football in 2007.

MIROSLAV  KLOSE

DOB: 09.06.1978

NATIONALITY: Germany

POSITION: Forward

CURRENT CLUB:
Bayern Munich

PREVIOUS CLUBS:
Werder Bremen, Kaiserslautern, FC Homburg

The Bayern Munich and Germany striker turned 32 ahead of the World Cup in 2010, but he still showed the predatory instincts and aerial ability that have made him one of the world's deadliest frontmen. The 2010/11 season was his fourth with Bayern. He was top scorer in 2008/09 with 20 goals in all competitions, then helped them win the Bundesliga and finish runners-up in the Champions League a season later. Klose has a proud record in major tournaments, finishing top scorer at the 2006 World Cup with five goals. He is second only to Gerd Muller in Germany's all-time scoring charts.

LUCIO

DOB: 08.05.1978

NATIONALITY: Brazil

POSITION: Defence

CURRENT CLUB:
Inter Milan

PREVIOUS CLUBS:
Bayern Munich,
Bayer Leverkusen,
Internacional

The Brazilian's appearance at the World Cup in 2010 was his third in the competition – his first as captain – but his side's elimination against Holland in the quarter-finals prevented him from lifting the trophy. It was a rare occurrence of being on the losing side. The Inter Milan captain lifted three trophies in 2009/10, bagged the World Cup in 2002, collected nine winners' medals in five years with Bayern Munich and scored the winning goal in the 2009 Confederations Cup final. An excellent reader of the game, he is also comfortable with the ball at his feet.

RUUD
VAN NISTELROOY

DOB: 01.07.1976

NATIONALITY: Holland

POSITION: Forward

CURRENT CLUB:
Malaga CF

PREVIOUS CLUBS:
Hamburg, Real Madrid,
Manchester United, PSV
Eindhoven, Heerenveen,
Den Bosch,

Sir Alex Ferguson waited a year to land the Dutch international after he got injured on the verge of signing for Manchester United, so their fans expected something special when he finally arrived in 2001. His record at previous club PSV Eindhoven, where he scored 62 goals in 67 games, suggested a glittering career ahead. His sensational record continued for Manchester United. He scored 95 in 150 games before moving to Real Madrid, where he bagged a further 46 in 68 and almost single-handedly won them the league title in his first season. In 2010 he joined Hamburg before signing for Malaga in Spain in 2011.

ANDREA PIRLO

LEGEND

DOB:	19.05.1979
NATIONALITY:	Italy
POSITION:	Midfield

CURRENT CLUB:
Juventus

PREVIOUS CLUBS:
AC Milan, Brescia (loan),
Reggina (loan),
Inter Milan, Brescia

Now in his 30s, Pirlo remains a key player for club and country. A deep-lying playmaker, he was once described as "Zico in front of the defence" by former Brazil coach Carlos Alberto Parreira, but he can also play in a more advanced position where his vision, exceptional passing and ability to shoot from distance make him an obvious danger. He occupies the more advanced position for Italy, for whom he has assumed the captain's armband. He was a World Cup winner in 2006 and he won two Champions League titles and two Scudettos with AC Milan before joining Juventus in 2011.

CARLES PUYOL

DOB: 13.04.1978

NATIONALITY: Spain

POSITION: Defence

CURRENT CLUB:
Barcelona

PREVIOUS CLUBS:
n/a

A first-choice option for club and country, the 32-year-old Spanish defender is a defensive rock who has enjoyed incredible success. As Barcelona captain he lifted six titles in 2009: La Liga, the Copa del Rey, the Spanish Super Cup, the Champions League, the European Super Cup and the FIFA Club World Cup. This was sandwiched between winning the European Championship in 2008 and World Cup in 2010 with Spain. Despite starting life as a winger, the mop-haired defender has forged a career at the back where his strength, heading ability and persistence make him one of the world's best.

RAUL

DOB: 27.06.1977

NATIONALITY: Spain

POSITION: Forward

CURRENT CLUB:
Schalke

PREVIOUS CLUBS:
Real Madrid

The all-time leading goalscorer at the world's most famous club, Schalke striker Raul will always be synonymous with Spanish giants Real Madrid. Sharp, intelligent and deadly in the box in his 18-year stay at the Bernabeu, Raul won six La Liga titles and the Champions League three times in five years. A host of individual accolades also came his way before he left Madrid to join Schalke having scored 228 league goals in 550 games. 'Raul is still the king' cried one Spanish newspaper after he scored against Deportivo La Coruna on the opening day of the 2009/10 season – to Madrid fans, he will always reign supreme.

RONALDO

LEGEND

DOB: 22.09.1976

NATIONALITY: Brazil

POSITION: Forward

CURRENT CLUB:
Corinthians

PREVIOUS CLUBS:
AC Milan, Real Madrid,
Inter Milan, Barcelona,
PSV Eindhoven, Cruzeiro

Although Ronaldo retired from the game in February 2011, he had continued to dazzle and find the net with alarming regularity in his final season. Before calling time on his glittering career he managed to fire in 18 goals in 31 games for Corinthians yet remarkably his statistics at previous clubs are even better. He scored 42 times in 45 games at PSV Eindhoven, 34 in 37 for Barcelona, 49 in 68 for Inter Milan, 82 in 127 for Real Madrid and nine in 20 for AC Milan. He has scored more World Cup goals (15) than anyone in the history of the game.

RONALDINHO

DOB: 21.03.1980

NATIONALITY: Brazil

POSITION: Forward

CURRENT CLUB:
AC Milan

PREVIOUS CLUBS:
Barcelona, Paris
Saint-Germain, Gremio

The former World Player of the Year hadn't played international football since April 2009 until he was recalled by new Brazil coach Mano Menezes in November 2010. Popular playmaker Ronaldinho had impressed with a series of strong displays for AC Milan. The Brazilian can play on the wing or behind the attackers and in 2009/10 he made 13 assists, the highest in Serie A. He won his first Serie A winners' medal with the Rossoneri in 2011, which he adds to the World Cup and Confederations Cup titles he won with Brazil, as well as the Champions League and two La Liga winners' medals he collected at Barcelona.

MARCOS SENNA

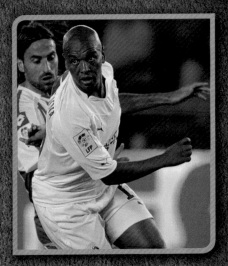

DOB: 17.07.1976

NATIONALITY: Spain

POSITION: Midfield

CURRENT CLUB:
Villarreal

PREVIOUS CLUBS:
Sao Caetano, Juventude,
Corinthians, America-SP,
Rio Branco

The Spaniard missed out on a place in the Spanish national team in the World Cup in 2010, but he remains a key player for Villarreal. His best year so far was 2008. He scored the "best goal" of his life from the centre circle in a game against Real Betis and netted a further three goals as his team finished a club-best second in La Liga. That summer, he was instrumental as Spain lifted the European Championship. His incisive passing and ability to stop opposing attacks made him the perfect foil for the more creative attacking players.

PAUL
SCHOLES

DOB: 16.11.1974

NATIONALITY: England

POSITION: Midfield

CURRENT CLUB:
Manchester United

PREVIOUS CLUBS:
n/a

Paul Scholes' form in 2009/10 saw Fabio Capello ask him to come out of international retirement for the World Cup in South Africa. Scholes declined, but he started 2010/11 in inspirational form. He made two assists as Manchester United won their season opener, scored his 150th United goal a week later and collected his tenth Premier League winners' medal in May. Popular with United fans and considered the best in the business by many of his peers, Scholes boasts the fourth-highest number of appearances in the club's history but retired in May 2011.

FRANCESCO TOTTI

DOB: 27.09.1976

NATIONALITY: Italy

POSITION: Forward

CURRENT CLUB:
AS Roma

PREVIOUS CLUBS:
n/a

One-club man and World Cup-winner Francesco Totti continues to lead hometown side Roma with distinction, wearing the captain's armband and posing a threat as either the second striker or in an attacking midfield position. He is contracted to the club until 2014, at which point he will be become a director for a further five years. First, though, he will endeavour to win a second Serie A title and climb above fifth-placed Roberto Baggio in the list of all-time Serie A goalscorers. Totti has been a league runner-up six times since winning the Scudetto in 2001.

EDWIN
VAN DER SAR

DOB: 29.10.1970

NATIONALITY: Holland

POSITION: Goalkeeper

CURRENT CLUB:
Manchester United

PREVIOUS CLUBS:
Fulham, Juventus, Ajax

The 2010/11 campaign was Van der Sar's 21st – and last – season as a first-team goalkeeper. During the 2009/10 season, aged 39, he overcame a broken finger and a knee injury to perform heroics for Manchester United and was rewarded with a contract extension. A year earlier he had been named UEFA goalkeeper of the year – 14 years after winning it for the first time, in 1995 – having kept 21 clean sheets and setting a world top-flight record of 1,311 minutes without conceding in the 2008/09 season. He signed off at Old Trafford with his fourth Premier League winners' medal. Holland's most-capped player, he came out of international retirement during qualification for the 2010 World Cup.

JAVIER ZANETTI

DOB: 10.08.1973

NATIONALITY: Argentina

POSITION: Midfield

CURRENT CLUB:
Inter Milan

PREVIOUS CLUBS:
Banfield, Talleres RE

The most-capped player in Argentine history and second behind Giuseppe Bergomi in Inter Milan's all-time appearances list, Zanetti continues to be influential for club and country. He won the treble with Inter Milan in 2009/10, the last leg of which – the Champions League final – was his 700th game for the club. He was left out of the World Cup squad but was recalled to the Argentina set-up in September 2010 for a game against Spain, before which he was recognised by the Argentine FA with an award for his outstanding career. He can play in the centre of midfield, on either wing or at full-back.

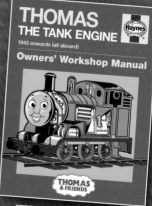